Cotswold Rid

by
Sheila Booth

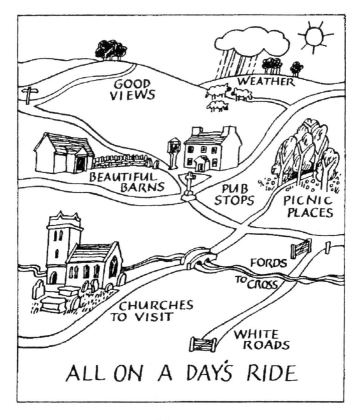

ALL ON A DAY'S RIDE

Maps

All the rides have a very good sketch map but a copy of an O.S. may prove useful, they are all on Ordnance Survey Touring Map and Guide 8. The Cotswolds (1"= 1 mile: 1.6cm = 1km) except the western edge of the Nailsworth, Avening and Chavenage ride.

1

Published
by
REARDON PUBLISHING
56, Upper Norwood Street, Lechampton,
Cheltenham, Glos, GL53 0DU

Copyright 1997
Reardon & Son

Written and Researched
by
Sheila Booth

ISBN 1 873877 23 4

Layout & Design
Nicholas Reardon

Maps & Illustrations
Peter T Reardon

Outside cover photos
by W. D. M. Price
All other photos by
Nicholas Reardon

Printed by
STOATE & BISHOP (Printers) Ltd
Cheltenham, Glos

Introduction

This book of Cotswold cycle rides is designed for families, but the rides can be enjoyed by anyone who would like a short ride in the countryside.

Most rides are between 10 and 15 miles long, and all can be ridden in an afternoon or a morning. They are on quiet country roads, though some go across classified roads or have a short stretch along one; one or two rides have a short stretch on a bridle path.

Many rides have something which will particularly appeal to children - a ford, a park, an interesting feature. All the rides pass at least one pub so that it is possible to stop for refreshments; and most of the rides have at least one shop on the route

The easy rides are mainly those in the south; some are virtually flat, and others have some minor hills. The undulating rides have some longer or slightly steeper hills, but most people should find them fairly easy even though they may need to walk a short stretch. The hilly rides have some long and/or steep hills - and of course they also have some downhills!

What to wear and take with you

It is not necessary to buy specialised cycling clothes. It is a good idea to wear/take:

Trousers which are easy to move in but fairly close to the leg below the knee - leggings are ideal - this stops the trousers catching the chain. If you haven't got narrow legged trousers a rubber band will hold them in. You can wear jeans but if they are tight they will be difficult to cycle in. Shoes with a firm, flat sole so that you will be able to exert pressure on the pedals easily. A warm jacket, and something waterproof. Gloves to keep your hands warm and protect them. A helmet, but it is not a legal requirement. Wear bright clothing. Carry a pump, a spare inner tube, lights and a small tool kit - something to eat - chocolate, bananas - a small first aid kit. Pack items that you are carrying carefully - loose items can be dangerous.

Check your cycle over before you set out and make sure that the brakes, gears, etc are working properly and that your tyres are blown up. Obey the Highway Code. Ride in single file on narrow or busy roads. Watch out for potholes and poor edges to the roads, and warn the other riders about them.

KEYNES COUNTRY PARK, EWEN AND SHORNCOTE

Distance = 8.6 miles / 13.7 km   Terrain * easy

This easy ride starts in Keynes Country Park where you can picnic and paddle. The ride goes to Ewen and Shorncote along quiet, level, country roads.

Turn left out of Keynes Country Park (1) and after 0.4m turn right signed Somerford Keynes. As the road turns left to the Spine Road turn right again signed Somerford Keynes. Turn right in Somerford Keynes (2) signed Siddington, and just out of the village turn left signed Ewen, and follow the lane for 1.4m to Ewen. [2.9m/4.6km]

Turn left in Ewen signed Kemble, and then right signed Siddington. Follow this lane for 2m, then turn left signed Cirencester and first right signed Siddington. After 0.4m turn right along Upper Siddington signed 'Weak Bridge'. [2.6m/4.1km]

Over the old canal, and at the T junction turn right and first left - unsigned. At the next T junction turn right (with care - relatively busy road) and first left signed Shorncote. Through the hamlet of Shorncote (3), and at the next junction turn left and back to the Country Park (1) on the left. [3.1m/5km]

INFORMATION

1. KEYNES COUNTRY PARK   This park has boats, picnic and BBQ sites, an adventure playground and a children's beach.   [T]

2. SOMERFORD KEYNES   Somerford refers to a ford through the Thames, and the name appears in a Saxon charter of 685.   The church dates back to the C8th, and inside the door recess there is an C11th stone carving of the heads of two dragons both biting a ball.   [Ch PH]

3. SHORNCOTE   This hamlet was once a mediaeval manor and therefore had its own church. There is a late Norman chancel arch and the remains of C12th wall paintings in the chancel. The double bellcote is C14th.   [Ch]

Other PHs: Ewen. Shop; Siddington.

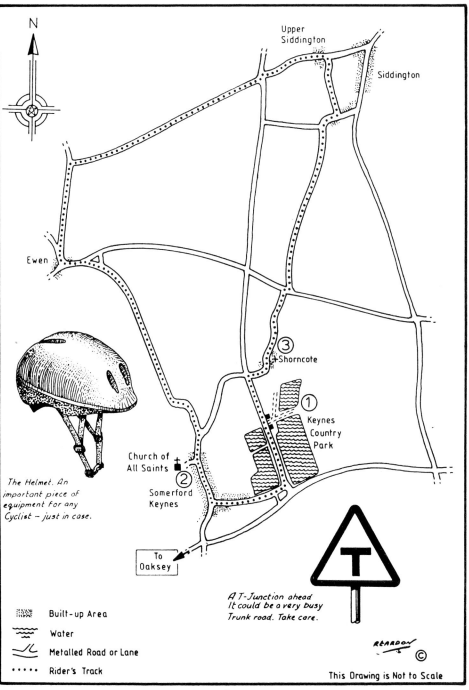

N

Upper Siddington

Siddington

Ewen

③ +Shorncote

① Keynes Country Park

Church of All Saints +

② Somerford Keynes

The Helmet. An important piece of equipment for any Cyclist – just in case.

To Oaksey

A T-Junction ahead It could be a very busy Trunk road. Take care.

T

REARDON ©

This Drawing is Not to Scale

Built-up Area

Water

Metalled Road or Lane

Rider's Track

FAIRFORD, DOWN AMPNEY AND POULTON

Distance = 13.3 miles / 21.3 km Terrain * easy

This is an easy, level ride to the West of Fairford. Fairford church is worth spending time in - there are wonderful stained glass windows.

Going East through Down Ampney (1) turn left signed Poulton. At A417 in Poulton turn right then first left up Bell Lane signed Bibury. After 0.6m turn right at Betty's Grave X roads, and then right again at Sunhill X roads along Welsh Way (2) to/signed Fairford. On the outskirts of Fairford turn right at T junction and first left - you will pass a pretty pond. In Fairford (3) turn right just after the church into the Market Place. [6.8m/10.9km]

Leave Fairford on A417 towards Cirencester and after 0.6m turn left just after an electricity sub station - no sign. Go straight over next X roads, and left at T junction - both signed Marston Meysey - to Marston Meysey. [3.9m/6.3km]

Through Marston Meysey and at T junction turn right signed Cricklade and next right signed Down Ampney. Continue along this road for 2m back to Down Ampney (1) (ignoring sign to right to Down Ampney Estate). [2.6m/4.1km]

INFORMATION

1. DOWN AMPNEY   Neither the village nor church is typical of the Cotswolds. The church has white walls with red flowers first painted on the arcades in the C13th, and an RAF memorial window in the north wall. [Ch Sh]

2. WELSH WAY   Before the railways Welsh drovers used this road to drive cattle to the London markets.

3. FAIRFORD   is an attractive market town. The church is one of the Cotswold wool churches: it was built in the early C16th, and paid for by the Tame family, wealthy wool merchants. The stained glass windows are famous; there are also lovely wood carvings, brasses and stone sculptures. [C Ch PH Sh T Ts]

Other PHs: Marston Meysey; Poulton. Other shops: Poulton

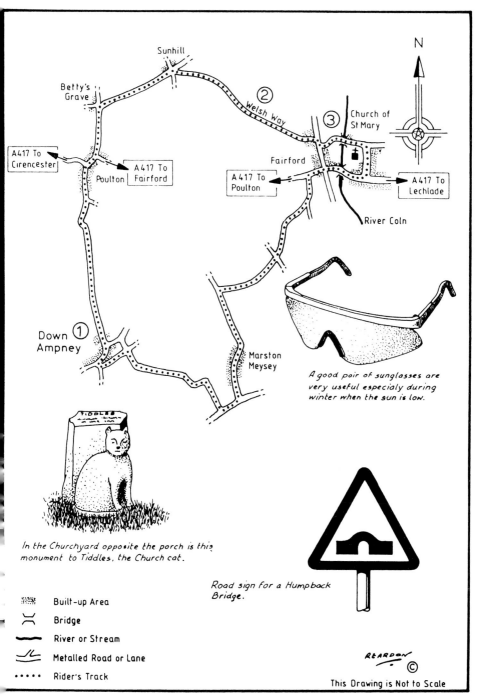

N

Sunhill

Betty's
Grave

② Welsh Way

③ Church of
St Mary

A417 To
Cirencester

A417 To
Poulton

A417 To
Fairford

Fairford

A417 To
Poulton

A417 To
Lechlade

River Coln

Down
Ampney ①

Marston
Meysey

A good pair of sunglasses are very useful especialy during winter when the sun is low.

TIDDLES

In the Churchyard opposite the porch is this monument to Tiddles, the Church cat.

Road sign for a Humpback Bridge.

▦ Built-up Area

╳ Bridge

▬ River or Stream

〜 Metalled Road or Lane

••••• Rider's Track

REARDON ©

This Drawing is Not to Scale

AMPNEY CRUCIS, BETTY'S GRAVE, BARNSLEY WOLD AND BARNSLEY

Distance = 12.5 miles / 20 km   Terrain ** undulating

This gently undulating ride covers some attractive Cotswold countryside along quiet lanes. There are two attractive villages - Barnsley and Ampney Crucis.

Go through Ampney Crucis (1) village to the East, and at the T junction turn right signed Poulton and first left signed Ampney St. Mary. In Ampney St Mary bear right at the fork (unsigned), and left at the T junction (unsigned), and along this road for 0.5m to Betty's Grave (2) X roads. [2.8m/4.5km]

Turn left at Betty's Grave signed Ready Token. After 1.5m go straight over at Ready Token (3) X roads signed Arlington, and continue to B4425. [2.8m/4.5km]

At B4425 junction go over and bear left signed Foss Cross, and follow this lane for 2m to X roads. Turn left here signed Barnsley, and at the T junction after 0.9m turn left again signed Barnsley. [2.7m/4.3km]

You will pass Barnsley Wold on the left. After 1.5m turn left and left again at the gate on the corner of Barnsley Park and into Barnsley (4). Turn right along B4425 in the village, and just outside turn left signed Ampney Crucis. After 1.9m turn right back into Ampney Crucis (1). [4.2m/6.7km]

INFORMATION

1. AMPNEY CRUCIS   The village has a famous old cross, 13ft high, with a gabled top with a crucifixion. The church has a fine Norman chancel arch, a C15th stone pulpit, and a fascinating tomb with the life size figures of George Lloyd, his wife and five sons and seven daughters. [Ch PH Sh]

2. BETTY'S GRAVE   but who was Betty?

3. READY TOKEN so called because the coachmen had to have their tolls ready.

4. BARNSLEY   The village has a beautiful church with Norman carvings, & many other interesting features. Barnsley House Garden is open to the public with admission charge. [Ch G PH]

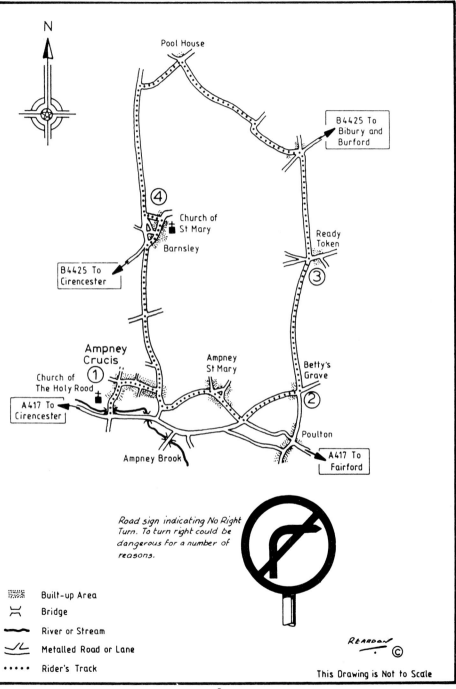

N

Pool House

B4425 To Bibury and Burford

④ Church of St Mary

Barnsley

B4425 To Cirencester

Ready Token

③

Ampney Crucis

① Ampney St Mary

Betty's Grave

Church of The Holy Rood

② A417 To Cirencester

Poulton

A417 To Fairford

Ampney Brook

Road sign indicating No Right Turn. To turn right could be dangerous for a number of reasons.

Built-up Area

Bridge

River or Stream

Metalled Road or Lane

Rider's Track

REARDON ©

This Drawing is Not to Scale

9

BARNSLEY, THE COLN VALLEY AND BIBURY

Distance = 13.1 miles / 21 km   Terrain ** undulating

This attractive ride on quiet country roads goes through Barnsley and Bibury and down the Coln Valley. It is a gently undulating ride through several beautiful villages. There are interesting churches at Coln Rogers and Barnsley, and many things to see and do in Bibury.

In Barnsley (1) cycle along B4425 in the direction of Bibury, and take the unsigned left turn after the Village Pub and near the 40mph sign just before the B4425 turns right. Turn right at the T junction near a gated entrance to Barnsley Park (no sign), and continue along this road to Coln Rogers. [3.2m/5.1km].

At Coln Rogers T junction turn left to the village and the church (2); then return and cycle over the River Coln and follow this road to Winson. In Winson turn left signed Winson village; through the village and left just after the church to Ablington. In Ablington outskirts turn left and cross the river. Turn right at the next T junction, and follow signs to Bibury (3). [2.8m/4.5km].

Leave Bibury on B4425 towards Burford and as you leave the village turn right on a blind corner - with care - signed Coln St. Aldwyns. In Coln St. Aldwyns (4) outskirts turn right at T junction into the village. [2.5m/4km]

Leave Coln St. Aldwyns towards Quenington, cross the River Coln and turn right at the top of the hill along Coneygar Road, signed Barnsley. Just past the X roads in the hamlet of Ready Token (5) turn right, signed Barnsley. When you reach the B4425 turn left back into Barnsley (1). [4.6m/7.4km].

INFORMATION

1. BARNSLEY is a quiet village with a beautiful church with Norman carvings, and many other interesting features. Barnsley House Garden is interesting and is open to the public. [Ch PH]

2. COLN ROGERS' church has an almost intact Saxon nave and chancel.   [Ch]

3. BIBURY is a beautiful, popular village on the River Coln. Arlington Row is a C17th row of weavers' cottages, and Arlington Mill a C17th corn mill with working machinery. The church has Saxon, Norman and later work, and the churchyard has well carved table tombs with 'bale' tops.   [C Ch M PH Sh T Ts]

4. COLN ST. ALDWYNS is a very pretty village with an Elizabethan Manor House. The church has a Norman doorway, and gargoyles.   [C Ch PH Sh]

5. READY TOKEN so called because the coachmen had to have their tolls ready.

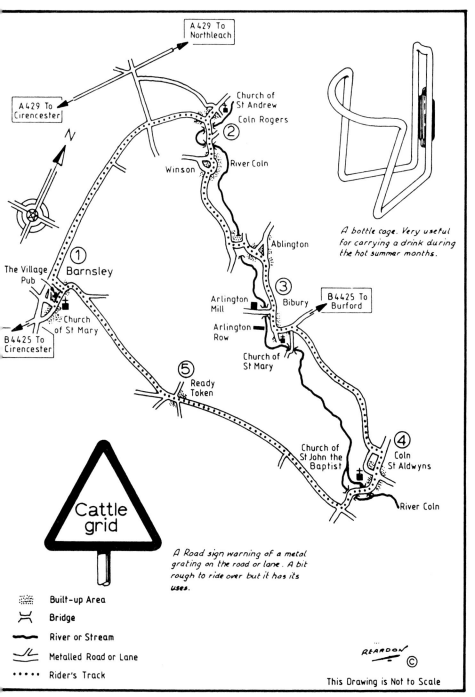

A429 To
Northleach

A429 To
Cirencester

N

Church of
St Andrew

Coln Rogers

②

River Coln

Winson

The Village
Pub

① Barnsley

Church
of St Mary

B4425 To
Cirencester

Ablington

Arlington
Mill

③ Bibury

B4425 To
Burford

Arlington
Row

Church of
St Mary

⑤ Ready
Token

Church of
St John the
Baptist

④ Coln
St Aldwyns

River Coln

A bottle cage. Very useful
for carrying a drink during
the hot summer months.

Cattle
grid

A Road sign warning of a metal
grating on the road or lane. A bit
rough to ride over but it has its
uses.

Built-up Area

Bridge

River or Stream

Metalled Road or Lane

Rider's Track

REARDON ©

This Drawing is Not to Scale

11

KEMBLE, OAKSEY, CRUDWELL AND KEMBLE WICK

Distance = 11.7 miles / 18.7 km Terrain * easy

This easy ride at the Western edge of the Water Park goes along quiet country lanes. There is a short stretch of bridlepath near Kemble Wick.

From Kemble (1) cycle to the East over A429 and the next minor X roads; as the through road bears left keep straight on along Washpool Lane signed Poole Keynes. After 0.7m turn right at T junction signed Poole Keynes, and follow the road to Poole Keynes. Go straight through, and left at the next T junction, both signed Oaksey; and in Oaksey (2) turn right along The Street. [3.5m/5.6km]

Through Oaksey and at the end of the village turn left opposite the Post Office signed Eastcourt. At Eastcourt X roads after 0.8m turn right, and follow this lane for 1.4m to Crudwell. [2.7m/4.3km]

Turn left along A429 in Crudwell, and then right after 0.1m just after the Mayfield House Hotel. Go through the old ford, or along the path to its right, and then turn right. Follow this lane for 1.7m to T junction and turn right and continue to A429. [2.5m/4km]

Straight over A429 signed Oaksey, and after 0.7m where Chelworth is signed to right turn left up the bridlepath signed Kemble Wick. Pass Woodlands Farm on the right and then left up the lane to Kemble Wick. Turn left in Kemble Wick and over the railway line back to Kemble (1). [3m/4.8km]

INFORMATION

1. KEMBLE   The station is on the Swindon to Cheltenham line. The tunnel as the train comes into Kemble from Swindon is a memento to Anna Gordon who insisted on its construction so that the railway was screened from Kemble house.   [Ch PH Sh]

2. OAKSEY   The church has ancient wall paintings.   [Ch PH Sh]

Other PH and Sh: Crudwell.

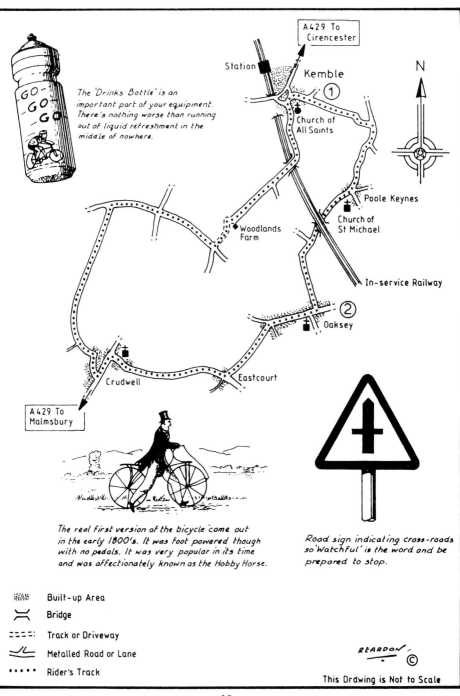

A429 To
Cirencester

Station

Kemble
①

Church of
All Saints

N

The 'Drinks Bottle' is an
important part of your equipment.
There's nothing worse than running
out of liquid refreshment in the
middle of nowhere.

GO
GO
GO

Poole Keynes

Church of
St Michael

Woodlands
Farm

In-service Railway

② Oaksey

Crudwell

Eastcourt

A429 To
Malmsbury

The real first version of the bicycle came out
in the early 1800's. It was foot powered though
with no pedals. It was very popular in its time
and was affectionately known as the Hobby Horse.

Road sign indicating cross-roads
so 'Watchful' is the word and be
prepared to stop.

	Built-up Area
	Bridge
::::::	Track or Driveway
⌐	Metalled Road or Lane
•••••	Rider's Track

REARDON ©

This Drawing is Not to Scale

NAILSWORTH, AVENING AND CHAVENAGE

Distance = 11.5 miles / 18.4 km   Terrain *** hilly

This attractive ride on country roads and lanes starts with an easy climb, and has a flat section around Chavenage. The return journey has some steep hills and blind corners which need care.

From Nailsworth (1) Old Market turn right down Spring Hill to the round-about: turn right up A46 and first left along Tabrams Pitch, and continue along this road (B4014) beside the stream past the Weighbridge Inn to Avening. In Avening (2) go up the hill until the road turns right: turn left up Star Lane signed Culkerton. After 0.9m turn right at Star Farm signed Chavenage; cross B4014 signed Chavenage House; and continue for 0.6m to an unsigned T junction. [5.3m/8.5km]

You can turn left to Chavenage House (3), and return (0.5m): or turn R, and continue along this road for 1.8m to A46. Straight over A46 along Hazelcote Farm lane, past the farm, and at the first (unsigned) junction bear right - this lane will take you to Tiltups End Inn. Turn sharp left at the PH along Hay Lane, signed 'unsuitable for heavy vehicles' - be careful! there is a steep downhill on this stretch - at the bottom go over the bridge, and up the hill to the PH in Horsley. [4.5m/7.2km]

Turn right down B4058, and immediately left signed Downend: and at the next junction bear left signed Shortwood. Up the hill, and right at the junction (unsigned), then right at the next junction signed Shortwood. After 0.4m - as the lane bears left into Homefield and a housing estate - bear right past a bollard down a tarmacked path which becomes Ragnall Lane. Turn right at the bottom, and follow the road for 0.3m to junction with Newmarket Road in Nailsworth. Turn right and back to Old Market. [1.7m/2.7km]

INFORMATION

1. NAILSWORTH   A former cloth town linked with Stroud by the old railway track (now the cycletrack) and the river, along which there are many attractive old mills. [C Ch PH Sh T Ts TIC]
2. AVENING   The village is situated in a valley. The church is early Norman, and in the South transept there is a model of the Avening Long Barrow (a burial chamber), and models of the church at various stages in its development. [Ch PH Sh T]
3. CHAVENAGE HOUSE   An Elizabethan Manor House (1576) open to the public with admission charge. Other PHs: Weighbridge (on road to Avening); Tiltups End on A46; Horsley.

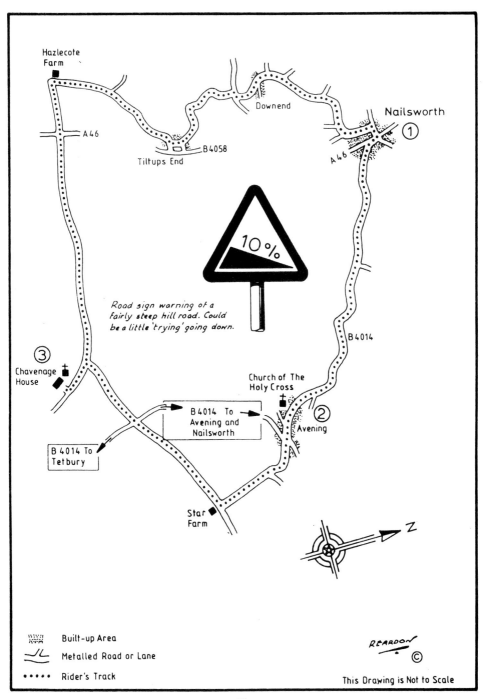

Hazlecote Farm

A46

Tiltups End   B4058

Downend

Nailsworth ①

A46

10 %

Road sign warning of a fairly steep hill road. Could be a little 'trying' going down.

③
Chavenage House

B4014

Church of The Holy Cross

B4014 To Avening and Nailsworth

② Avening

B4014 To Tetbury

Star Farm

Z

Built-up Area

Metalled Road or Lane

Rider's Track

REARDON ©

This Drawing is Not to Scale

15

CHERINGTON LAKE, ASHLEY POND AND TETBURY

Distance = 12.4 miles / 19.8 km   Terrain * easy

This attractive ride on quiet country roads goes to Cherington lake (where you could picnic), to Ashley pond, and into Tetbury where there are shops and cafes. It is an easy ride over fairly level countryside - except the short hill between Cherington and the lake.

From Tetbury (1) go down Chipping Street (next to Snooty Fox Hotel) - you will pass the Chipping Steps on your right. After 1m go straight over A433, signed Cherington. Continue along this road for 2.8m to Cherington. In Cherington (2) turn left at the green, just before the telephone box. Ignore the first right turn but take the second, signed Hampton Fields, and go down the steep hill. At the bottom there is a clearing on the left where you can get to the lake, or continue along the road up a short hill to a grassy area leading down to the lake. [4.4m/7km]

Return to Cherington village and turn left at the T jn opposite the green, and leave the village. On the outskirts keep straight on signed Rodmarton; after 0.9m at the next jn keep right signed Culkerton - you will go straight over A433. Just thro' Culkerton turn right, signed Ashley - note the pond on the left as you come into Ashley (3). [4m/6.4km]

Straight through Ashley and follow this road for 1.8m to Chedglow T junction: turn right signed Long Newnton. At Long Newnton T junction turn left, and at the B4014 T junction turn right and into Tetbury (1). [4m/6.4km]

INFORMATION

1. TETBURY   A prosperous market town with many handsome houses built by Wool Merchants in C17th and C18th. The C17th Market House was used for wool trading. The elegant parish church is C18th 'Gothic Revival'. There are many shops, cafes and pubs here. [C Ch PH Sh T Ts TIC]

2. CHERINGTON   A small quiet village with a large green which has a Victorian drinking fountain 'Let him that is athirst, come.'. The church has an Early English chancel and a Norman font. [Ch]

3. ASHLEY   A small village with a pond - note the duckhouse on stilts.

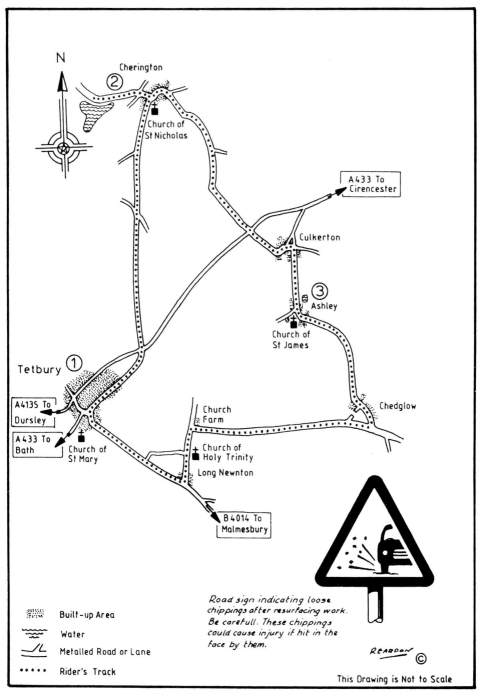

N

Cherington

②

Church of
St Nicholas

A433 To
Cirencester

Culkerton

③ Ashley

Church of
St James

Chedglow

Tetbury ①

A4135 To
Dursley

A433 To
Bath

Church of
St Mary

Church
Farm

Church of
Holy Trinity

Long Newnton

B4014 To
Malmesbury

Road sign indicating loose
chippings after resurfacing work.
Be carefull. These chippings
could cause injury if hit in the
face by them.

REARDON ©

This Drawing is Not to Scale

Built-up Area

Water

Metalled Road or Lane

Rider's Track

SAPPERTON, THE DUNTISBOURNES AND DAGLINGWORTH

Distance = 10.3 miles / 16.5 km   Terrain ** undulating

This lovely ride goes down the Dunt valley where there are fords in the villages. There is a Saxon church in Duntisbourne Rouse and Saxon sculptures in Daglingworth church - both make an interesting visit. There are refreshments at the pub in Sapperton.

From Sapperton church (1) go past the Bell inn to the T junction. Turn left here, signed Duntisbourne. After 1.2m at Park Corner keep straight on signed Winstone, and after 1.8m turn right at Jackbarrow Farm, signed Duntisbourne Abbots 1.0. [3.4m/5.4m]

Cycle along this road for 0.8m to the outskirts of Duntisbourne Abbots, and keep straight on (signed Birdlip), and in Duntisbourne Abbots (2) turn right down to the green and the ford. Turn right by the telephone box along road marked 'Ford' - the path goes alongside the long ford. At next T junction turn left to Duntisbourne Leer ford (3) - there are dovecotes in the walls of the houses. Return past the junction and further up the hill turn left to Middle Duntisbourne and Duntisbourne Rouse (4) - you can get down to the fords in both these villages. [2.7m/4.4km].

From Duntisbourne Rouse continue down to Daglingworth T junction (5), and turn left to the village and right at X roads to the church. Return to X roads and turn left and follow signs to Sapperton. Turn left at Park Corner, and after another 1.2m turn right into (signed) Sapperton (1). [4.2m/6.7km]

INFORMATION

1. SAPPERTON   The village was a centre of the Cotswold Arts and Crafts movement, and Gimson and the Barnsleys are buried in the churchyard. The church tower and spire are about 600 years old. [Ch PH]

2. DUNTISBOURNE ABBOTS   The village is on a slope round a green. There is a spring on the lower side from which the stream flows. The church has a beautiful late C12th font. The village is joined to Duntisbourne Leer by a long ford, which has a path alongside for walking and cycling. [Ch F]

3. DUNTISBOURNE LEER   The cottages near the ford have dovecotes in the walls. [F]

4. DUNTISBOURNE ROUSE   The cottages are near the ford. The village has an interesting church with some Saxon remains; the churchyard is entered along a grassy path, and there is a good view of the stream from the churchyard. [Ch F]

5. DAGLINGWORTH   A pretty village with the stream alongside the gardens. The church has a lot of Saxon work including the wall sculptures, the narrow doorway, and the tiny windows in the vestry wall. There are some interesting brass tablets in the floor of the porch.

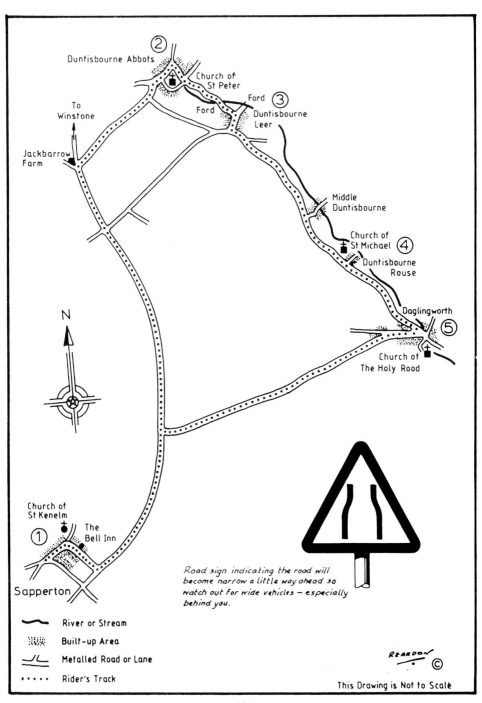

Duntisbourne Abbots
②
Church of
St Peter
Ford
Ford
③ Duntisbourne
Leer
To
Winstone
Jackbarrow
Farm
Middle
Duntisbourne
Church of
St Michael ④
Duntisbourne
Rouse
N
Daglingworth
⑤
Church of
The Holy Rood
Church of
St Kenelm
① The
Bell Inn
Sapperton

Road sign indicating the road will
become narrow a little way ahead so
watch out for wide vehicles — especially
behind you.

⌇⌇⌇ River or Stream	
░░░ Built-up Area	
⌐⌐ Metalled Road or Lane	
····· Rider's Track	

REARDON ©

This Drawing is Not to Scale

THE CANAL TUNNEL, COATES AND FRAMPTON MANSELL

Distance = 11 miles / 17.6 km   Terrain ** undulating

This interesting ride visits both ends of the two mile canal tunnel built to avoid the high ground between Coates and Sapperton. The ride is undulating with a steep hill down to (and up from!) the Daneway end of the tunnel.

From Frampton Mansell cycle towards Stroud. Straight over A419 X roads; after 0.8m keep straight on at X roads and after another 0.6m turn left signed Tarlton. On Tarlton outskirts turn left opposite water tower, and then left at the green in Tarlton signed Coates. After 0.6m turn left up a track signed Tunnel House to the eastern end of the canal tunnel (1). [5m/8km]

Return to the road and turn left to Coates. At Coates T junction turn left and follow the road through Coates (2) to A419, then turn left and first right signed Sapperton. Keep along this road for 1.6m over two minor X roads and down a steep hill to the canal bridge at Daneway. There is a path along to the right to the western end of the canal tunnel (1). [3.8m/6.1km]

Return to the road and back up the hill. At the X roads turn right and back to Frampton Mansell (or turn left into Sapperton (3) and return, then straight over X roads signed Frampton Mansell [+0.6m]). [2.2m/3.5km]

INFORMATION

1. CANAL TUNNEL This two mile long canal tunnel from Coates to Sapperton was built between 1784 and 1789 to negotiate the higher ground. The canal joined the Rivers Thames and Severn.
DANEWAY The entrance to the tunnel is along a path from the bridge over the canal. To the West the canal went down a long series of locks to Chalford. [PH]
COATES   The tunnel portal was restored in the 1960s. The Cotswold Canal Trust arranges Sunday afternoon boat trips into the tunnel in the winter - water level permitting. [PH]
2. COATES   The Norman church was refashioned in the C13th, and has a Norman font and priest's doorway. The nave wall has C16th and C17th brass inscriptions, and the stone seat round the West end of the South aisle supported the saying "the weakest may go to the wall". [Ch]
3. SAPPERTON   The village was closely associated with the Cotswold Arts and Crafts movement - members are buried in the churchyard. The church tower and spire are about 600 years old. [Ch PH] Other PHs: Frampton Mansell, Shop: A419 near Frampton Mansell

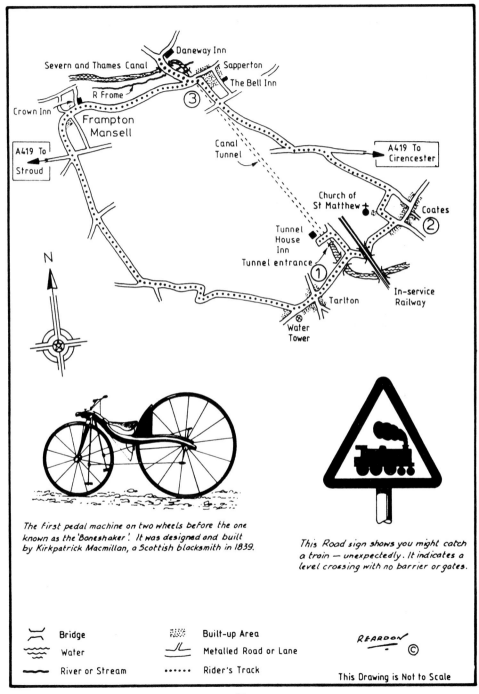

The first pedal machine on two wheels before the one known as the 'Boneshaker'. It was designed and built by Kirkpatrick Macmillan, a Scottish blacksmith in 1839.

This Road sign shows you might catch a train — unexpectedly. It indicates a level crossing with no barrier or gates.

Symbol	Legend
Bridge	
Water	
River or Stream	
Built-up Area	
Metalled Road or Lane	
Rider's Track	

REARDON ©

This Drawing is Not to Scale

THE EASTLEACHES, FILKINS, SHILTON AND WILD LIFE PARK

Distance = 12.9 miles / 20.7 km   Terrain ** undulating

This is a lovely ride in the Eastern Cotswolds through some beautiful villages which you will probably want to explore. There is an interesting working woollen mill in Filkins. The ride is fairly gentle.

From Eastleach Martin (1) take the road signed Filkins and continue for 2.2m. Turn right at the T junction, signed Lechlade, and almost immediately turn right again signed Filkins. Under the major road, and at Filkins T junction turn left to the Woollen Mill (2). [3.1m/5km]

Turn left out of the Woollen mill, and first right signed Broadwell. After 0.3m turn left at the X roads (no sign) and continue along this road for 1.1m going straight over Kencot X roads, and turn left signed Carterton. After 0.4m turn left again, signed Shilton, and follow this road for 2m to T junction - turn right here and down the hill into Shilton (3). [4.2m/6.7km]

From Shilton go back up the hill, straight over the T junction and over A361 X roads, both signed Holwell; the entrance to the Cotswold Wild Life Park (4) is on the left. Straight over the next three X roads, signed Eastleach / Eastleach Martin, and back to the Eastleaches (1). [5.6m/9km]

INFORMATION

1. EASTLEACH MARTIN and EASTLEACH TURVILLE Two lovely villages on opposite sides of the River Leach. There is an attractive stone footbridge over the river. Each village has a nice church; the Martin church has good examples of Decorated windows, and Mediaeval oak benches; the Turville church has a Norman doorway (Quenington school) and, inside, a lovely Early English chancel. [Ch PH]

2. FILKINS Cotswold Woollen Weavers have a working mill, with a wide range of cloths, clothes and rugs all woven from Cotswold wool. There is also an Exhibition, and a coffee shop. [C M Sh PH Ts]

3. SHILTON This pretty village has a marvellous ford - it is a good place to sit and paddle. [F PH]

4. COTSWOLD WILD LIFE PARK A collection of animals, birds, fish and reptiles in 120 acres of parkland. There is also a butterfly exhibition and a narrow gauge railway. [C Ts]

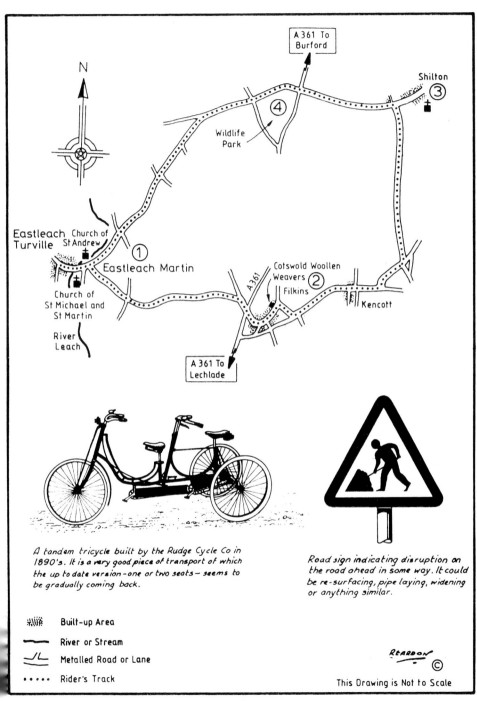

N

A 361 To
Burford

Shilton
③

④

Wildlife
Park

Eastleach
Turville

Church of
St Andrew

① Eastleach Martin

Cotswold Woollen
Weavers

A 361

Filkins

②

Kencott

Church of
St Michael and
St Martin

River
Leach

A 361 To
Lechlade

A tandem tricycle built by the Rudge Cycle Co in
1890's. It is a very good piece of transport of which
the up to date version – one or two seats – seems to
be gradually coming back.

Road sign indicating disruption on
the road ahead in some way. It could
be re-surfacing, pipe laying, widening
or anything similar.

꙾꙾꙾꙾   Built-up Area

River or Stream

Metalled Road or Lane

• • • •   Rider's Track

REARDON ©

This Drawing is Not to Scale

SHERBORNE, GREAT RISSINGTON AND WINDRUSH

Distance = 11.2 miles / 18 km Terrain ** undulating

This is a very pleasing ride over quiet, undulating countryside. There are beautiful villages, several relatively unknown, and a lovely Norman church in Windrush.

From Sherborne (1) go East through the village, and as the road turns sharp right turn left signed Clapton. Follow this quiet road up hill to Clapton-on-the-Hill. [3m/4.8km]

From Clapton return for 0.2m along the previous road, and then left down a road designated 'unsuitable for motors'. Down the hill and across River Windrush at New Bridge - there is a nice spot to picnic near the river. At the next T junction (unsigned) turn right to Great Rissington (2). [2.7m/4.3km]

Straight through Great Rissington and at the T junction after 0.5m turn right signed Great Barrington, and coast down hill to Great Barrington (3). [2.8m/4.5km].

Keep right in Great Barrington, cross the bridge, and take the next right turn, signed Sherborne. Follow this road to Windrush (4). From Windrush continue along the valley back to Sherborne (1). [2.7m/4.4km]

INFORMATION

1. SHERBORNE   The Eastern end of the village was built as a model estate village in the mid 1800s;   the Western end has some older cottages. The church has a mediaeval tower and spire, and several monuments to the Dutton family. Sherborne Park Estate is owned by the National Trust and there are marked walks in it. [Ch Sh]

2. GREAT RISSINGTON   The church, next to a manor house, has Norman foundations and arches. The church recently featured in the national press regarding a so-called 'Clochmerle' row about whether to install a lavatory for the use of playgroups etc. [Ch PH]

3. GREAT BARRINGTON   The village is on the Windrush River. The church has a lofty Norman chancel arch, and is next to the 'great house'. [Ch]

4. WINDRUSH   A pretty village with a picturesque church. It is particularly worth looking at the Norman South doorway which has two rows of beakheads. [Ch]
Other PHs: On the river after Great Barrington

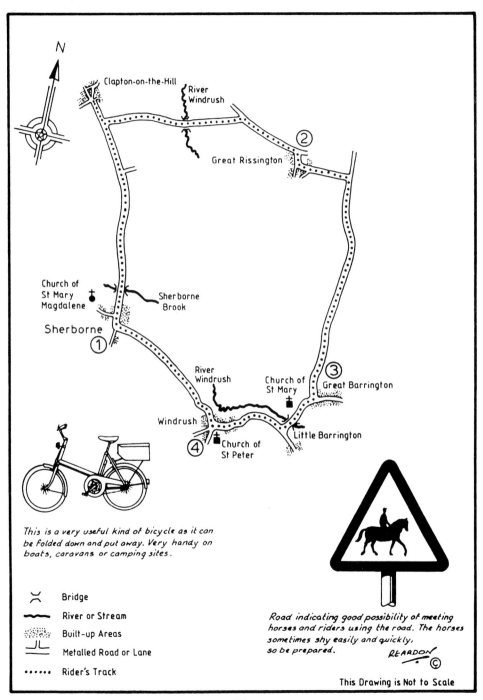

N

Clapton-on-the-Hill

River
Windrush

② Great Rissington

Church of
St Mary
Magdalene

Sherborne
Brook

Sherborne

①

River
Windrush

Church of
St Mary

③ Great Barrington

Windrush

Little Barrington

④ Church of
St Peter

This is a very useful kind of bicycle as it can
be folded down and put away. Very handy on
boats, caravans or camping sites.

⌣ Bridge

⌒ River or Stream

Built-up Areas

Metalled Road or Lane

•••••• Rider's Track

Road indicating good possibility of meeting
horses and riders using the road. The horses
sometimes shy easily and quickly,
so be prepared.

REARDON
©

This Drawing is Not to Scale

25

NORTHLEACH, SHERBORNE AND ALDSWORTH

Distance = 11.8 miles / 18.9 km Terrain *** hilly

This quiet rural ride starts and finishes in Northleach. The ride goes along the Sherborne Brook and beside Sherborne Park. It makes a lovely ride for a summer day.

Turn right out of Northleach (1) Market Square and after 0.1m turn left up Farmington Road signed Farmington. At the T junction after 1.3m turn right signed Farmington. Go straight through Farmington and along this road for 2m and straight over minor X roads signed Sherborne and into Sherborne (2). [4.6m/7.4km]

Turn right in Sherborne between a telephone box and the war memorial and just before the village shop. This partly tarmacked road goes up the Eastern side of Sherborne Park Estate to A40. Go straight over A40 signed Aldsworth, and follow this quiet road for 2.2m into Aldsworth (3) village. The PH is below the village on the B4425. [3.2m/5.1km]

To leave Aldsworth take the road signed Northleach and along this undulating road for 3.5m to the outskirts of Northleach. Turn left at T junction and back into Northleach (1). [4m/6.4km]

INFORMATION

1. NORTHLEACH   An important mediaeval Wool Centre with many attractive buildings. The church was paid for by Wool Merchants & has a famous collection of wool merchants' brasses. Just to the West of Northleach (0.2m) the Cotswold Countryside Collection Museum tells the story of Cotswold rural life. Admission charge. [C Ch M PH Sh T TIC Ts]

2. SHERBORNE   The Eastern end of the village was built as a model estate village in the mid 1800s; the Western end has some older cottages. The church has a mediaeval tower and spire, and several monuments to the Dutton family. Sherborne Park Estate is owned by the National Trust and there are marked walks in it. [Ch Sh]

3. ALDSWORTH   The church's North oak door was made by Norman craftsmen. Near the South porch are two scratch dials, one with 24 rays. [Ch PH]

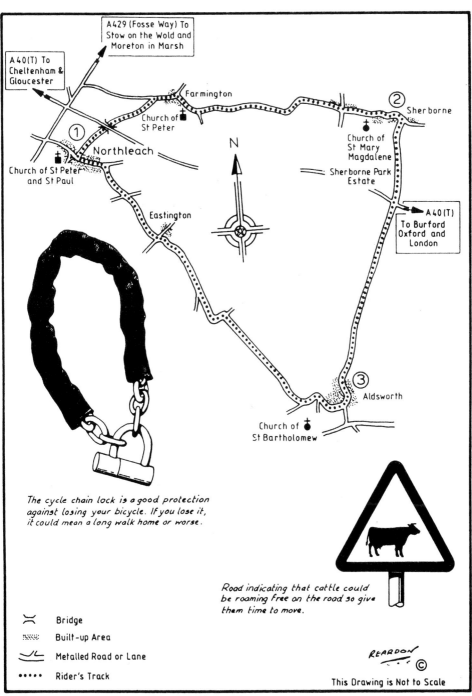

A429 (Fosse Way) To
Stow on the Wold and
Moreton in Marsh

A40(T) To
Cheltenham &
Gloucester

Farmington

Church of
St Peter

① Northleach

Church of St Peter
and St Paul

② Sherborne

Church of
St Mary
Magdalene

Sherborne Park
Estate

A40(T)
To Burford
Oxford and
London

N

Eastington

③ Aldsworth

Church of
St Bartholomew

The cycle chain lock is a good protection
against losing your bicycle. If you lose it,
it could mean a long walk home or worse.

Road indicating that cattle could
be roaming free on the road so give
them time to move.

⌣   Bridge

░░░   Built-up Area

⌣⌐   Metalled Road or Lane

•••••   Rider's Track

REARDON ©

This Drawing is Not to Scale

KINGHAM, BROADWELL AND ADLESTROP

Distance = 15.9 miles / 25.4 km   Terrain ** undulating

This pleasant ride over gently undulating countryside goes through several attractive villages just North East of Stow on the Wold. The ride is quiet and fairly easy, but with a steepish hill just out of Adlestrop.

From Kingham (1) go North and just outside the village turn left signed Daylesford and Stow. At A436 turn left, then take the 2nd right signed Broadwell, and into Broadwell (2) - there is a lovely green and fords here. [4.7m/7.5km]

From Broadwell turn left off the road you came in on, and follow signs to Evenlode (3). From Evenlode go back 0.7m down the previous road, and then turn left and follow signs to Adlestrop, turning right into the village by the old station sign (4). [4.4m/7km]

Go thro' Adlestrop village, turn right at T junction as you leave, and up the hill to T junction with A436. Turn left onto A436 and immediately right (no sign) and follow this road for 1.2m to Cornwell village on the left. [2.1m/3.4km]

From Cornwell continue along previous road (signed Chipping Norton) for 1.8m to X roads, and turn right along B4450 to Churchill (5). [3.2m/5.1km] In Churchill turn right down Kingham Road (signed Kingham 1.5) to Kingham (1). [1.5m/2.4km]

INFORMATION

1. KINGHAM has a large green. [Ch PH Sh]

2. BROADWELL is a pretty village with a large green beside a tributary of the river Evenlode. The church has many C17th table tombs. [Ch F PH]

3. EVENLODE is a quiet village. Its mediaeval church has a 'Sanctus chair' - one of only three in England - for those seeking sanctuary from trouble or persecution. [Ch]

4. ADLESTROP   As you enter the village stop at the bus shelter which has the old station sign, and a bench with Edward Thomas' poem about Adlestrop. The village is quiet and picturesque.

5. CHURCHILL   The unusual C19th Church is a scaled down version of Oxford buildings e.g. Magdalen Tower, Christ Church Hall roof. [Ch PH]

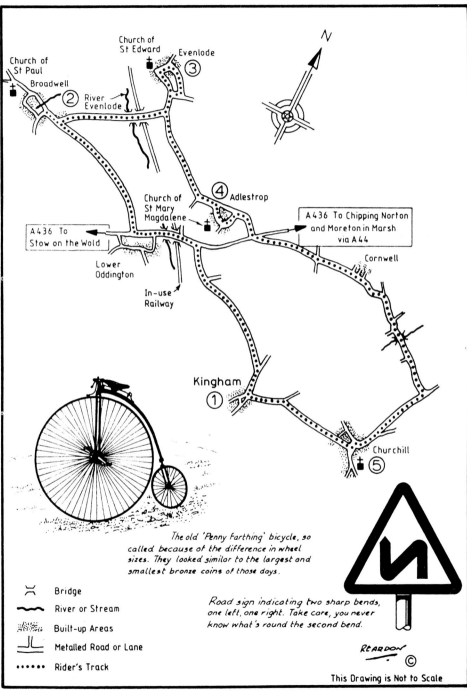

N

Church of
St Edward
Evenlode ③

Church of
St Paul
Broadwell ②

River
Evenlode

Church of
St Mary
Magdalene

④ Adlestrop

A436 To Chipping Norton
and Moreton in Marsh
via A44

A436 To
Stow on the Wold

Cornwell

Lower
Oddington

In-use
Railway

Kingham
①

Churchill
⑤

The old 'Penny Farthing' bicycle, so
called because of the difference in wheel
sizes. They looked similar to the largest and
smallest bronze coins of those days.

Bridge
River or Stream
Built-up Areas
Metalled Road or Lane
Rider's Track

Road sign indicating two sharp bends,
one left, one right. Take care, you never
know what's round the second bend.

REARDON ©

This Drawing is Not to Scale

BOURTON-ON-THE-WATER, THE SLAUGHTERS AND LOWER SWELL

Distance = 8.7 miles / 13.9 km Terrain ** undulating

This is a delightful short ride. Upper Slaughter is quiet; you can wade through the ford and sit on the banks of the stream. Lower Slaughter and Lower Swell are quiet and pretty. Bourton is busy with many things to do, and also has a nice green and a stream for paddling.

From Bourton (1) go along Lansdowne to A429. Turn right & immediately left, signed Naunton. Then turn right signed Lower Slaughter. After 0.6m take an unsigned right turn, and at the T junction at the bottom of the lane turn right into Lower Slaughter (2). [1.7m/2.7km]

To leave Lower Slaughter go over the bridge and left at the T junction and go along the road with the church on your right. Continue along this road for 2.2m to B4068, and turn right into Lower Swell (3). [2.4m/3.9km]

Leave Lower Swell towards Cheltenham and on the edge of the village turn left off B4068 signed The Slaughters. After 0.4m turn right signed Upper Slaughter. In Upper Slaughter (4) turn right just before the river along a road signed 'unsuitable for motors' to the green and the ford. [2.3m/3.7km]

Cross the ford and at the through road turn right. At the T junction after 0.1m turn left, then right opposite the hotel signed Bourton, and left at T junction after 0.4m signed Bourton. At A429 turn right and immediately left along Lansdowne into Bourton (1). [2.3m/3.6km]

INFORMATION

1. BOURTON ON THE WATER   This popular and pretty village is on the River Windrush. In the centre is a long green alongside the river, which can be crossed by several low bridges. There are several museums and many places for refreshment. [Ch F M PH Sh T Ts TIC]

2. LOWER SLAUGHTER   A beautiful village on the Windrush. It feels really peaceful and is worth walking round and looking at the Old Mill, cottages and the ducks. The manor house has a fine dovecote. [Ch Ts M]

3. LOWER SWELL   The village is on the River Dikler, a tributary of the Windrush. The War Memorial on the green was designed by Sir Edwin Lutyens. St. Mary's Church has Norman origins, see the carved chancel arch. [CH PH]

4. UPPER SLAUGHTER   A charming quiet village on the Windrush with bridges and a ford. There is a big sycamore over the stream, and a 17th century parsonage near the river; it is a nice place to picnic. The late Norman church has an attractive pinnacled tower; it was restored in the 1870s. The cottages on the right of the church were restored by Lutyens. [Ch F]

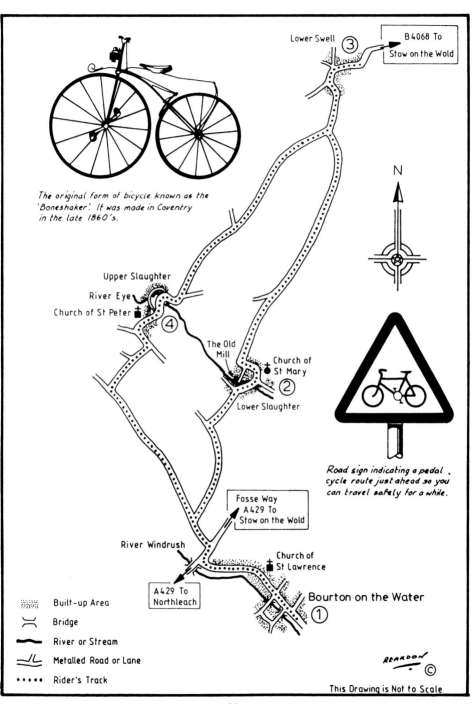

Lower Swell ③ → B 4068 To Stow on the Wold

N

The original form of bicycle known as the 'Boneshaker'. It was made in Coventry in the late 1860's.

Upper Slaughter
River Eye
Church of St Peter

④

The Old Mill

Church of St Mary

②

Lower Slaughter

Road sign indicating a pedal cycle route just ahead so you can travel safely for a while.

Fosse Way
A429 To
Stow on the Wold

River Windrush

Church of St Lawrence

A429 To Northleach

Bourton on the Water ①

	Built-up Area
⏝	Bridge
━	River or Stream
╩	Metalled Road or Lane
• • • • •	Rider's Track

REARDON ©

This Drawing is Not to Scale

NAUNTON, BROCKHAMPTON AND GUITING POWER

Distance = 13.6 miles / 21.8 km   Terrain *** hilly

This is a lovely ride on a fine day over the top of the Cotswolds and through some attractive villages. The ride is fairly hilly and there are some good views.

From Naunton (1) take the road to the West past the church to B4068, and turn right along it for 0.4m. Then bear right at Foxhill B&B through stone gateposts. Go past Tally Ho Farm, down and up a hill, and turn left at T junction, and along this road to Hawling (2). [3.6m/5.8km]

Turn left at the T junction after Hawling, signed Andoversford, and after 0.6m turn right at X rds and follow signs to Brockhampton. [2.8m/4.5km]

Turn right in the centre of Brockhampton (3) just after the phone box, and then left at each of the next two T junctions - the first signed to Guiting Power and the second to Roel. Turn right at Roel Gate X roads (4), and right at the next X roads, and follow signs to Guiting Power. [5m/8km]

Go straight through Guiting Power (5). At the T junction outside the village turn right, after 0.2m turn left, and after 0.3m turn right - all signed Naunton. Continue along this road for 0.6m and take an unsigned right turn just after Grange Hill Farm; go down the hill, and turn left into Naunton. [2.2m/3.5km]

INFORMATION

1. NAUNTON   A beautiful village with the long street parallel with the Windrush. There is fine stone dovecote with four gables near a barn, close to the pub. The church is a perpendicular 'wool' church, and has a C15th pulpit. [Ch D PH Sh]

2. HAWLING   There is a manor house. The church has a perpendicular tower, battlements and gargoyles; the lychgate is a peace memorial. [Ch]

3. BROCKHAMPTON   A linear village with an old pub. [PH]

4. ROEL GATE   This cross roads is 900ft above sea level.

5. GUITING POWER   A pretty village with cottages clustered round a green. The church has a Norman south doorway. [Ch PH Sh]

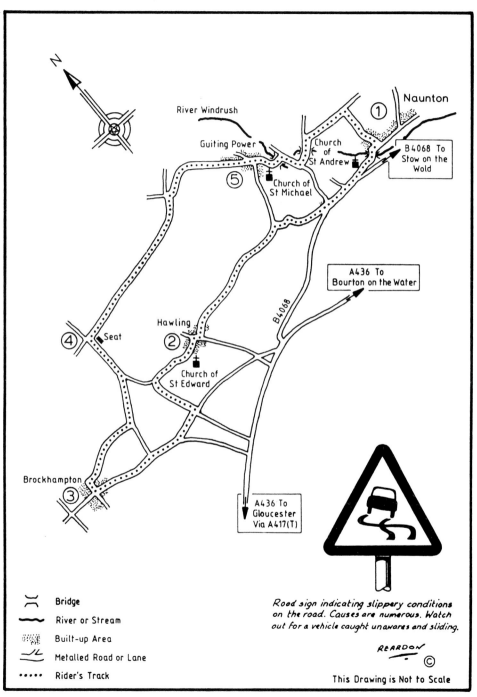

Legend:

- ⌣ Bridge
- ∿ River or Stream
- ▒ Built-up Area
- ∿ Metalled Road or Lane
- ••••• Rider's Track

Road sign indicating slippery conditions on the road. Causes are numerous. Watch out for a vehicle caught unawares and sliding.

REARDON ©

This Drawing is Not to Scale

CHIPPING CAMPDEN, EBRINGTON AND BROAD CAMPDEN

Distance = 13 miles / 20.7 km   Terrain *** undulating

This undulating ride starts and ends in Chipping Campden, a beautiful market town. It also goes through the quiet undulating countryside to the East, and visits several relatively unknown villages.

Leave Chipping Campden (1) on B4081 signed Mickleton, and after 1m turn right signed Hidcote, and right again signed Hidcote Gardens. Continue along this road for 1.6m to X roads and turn right signed Ebrington. Go straight over next X roads and at T junction bear left into Ebrington (2). [4.4m/7km].

From Ebrington take the road to the right of the PH signed Paxford. Go straight over B4035, and at B4479 T junction turn right into Paxford. In Paxford turn left signed Aston Magna, and then take the next left (unsigned). Follow this rural road for 2m, and turn right at T junction into Aston Magna. [3.7m/5.9km]

Continue through Aston Magna signed Draycott. In Draycott keep straight on at first junction, and then right, both signed Chipping Campden. At B4479 T junction turn right signed Paxford, and first left signed Broad Campden and follow this road for 1.6m into Broad Campden (3). Straight through Broad Campden signed Chipping Campden; turn right at B4081 back into Chipping Campden (1). [4.9m/7.8km]

INFORMATION

1. CHIPPING CAMPDEN   A very fine Cotswold Wool Town built by local craftsmen in local stone. The High Street is full of beautiful buildings, a C17th Market Hall along with near by C17th Almshouses. The lovely church is mainly C15th and has a stately tower with golden weathervanes; inside there are brasses and handsome monuments.   [Ch M PH Sh T TIC Ts]

2. EBRINGTON   The village is on a slope and has some thatched houses. The church is dedicated to St. Eadburgha - a Saxon saint. It has interesting contents including wall texts at the back of the nave with St. Paul's admonitions to husbands and wives. North of the altar there is a tomb chest with a large effigy of a Lord Chief Justice, and several monuments to the Keyte family. [Ch PH]

3. BROAD CAMPDEN   A very pretty, picture-postcard village. [Ch PH]

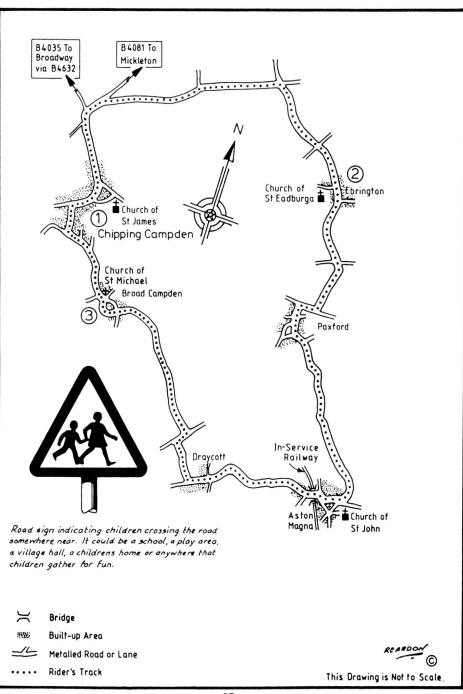

B4035 To Broadway via B4632

B4081 To Mickleton

N

Church of St Eadburga

② Ebrington

① Church of St James

Chipping Campden

Church of St Michael
Broad Campden

③

Paxford

Road sign indicating children crossing the road somewhere near. It could be a school, a play area, a village hall, a childrens home or anywhere that children gather for fun.

In-Service Railway

Draycott

Aston Magna

Church of St John

Bridge

Built-up Area

Metalled Road or Lane

Rider's Track

REARDON ©

This Drawing is Not to Scale.

TODENHAM, THE WOLFORDS AND CHERINGTON

Distance = 10.1 miles / 16.1 km   Terrain *** hilly

This quiet rural ride lies to the North East of Moreton in Marsh. It passes through several quiet villages and as you cycle you can often see the spire of the next church.

From Todenham (1) go North East signed Shipston on Stour. At A3400 turn left signed Shipston and immediately right signed Burmington. Turn right at Burmington outskirts signed Cherington, and follow this road for 1.9m to Cherington. Just over the bridge keep left - signed Whichford - into Cherington. [4.6m/7.4km]

In Cherington turn right just after PH up Featherbed Lane. Go right at the War Memorial, and continue along this road - signed Wolford - for 1.9m to A3400. Turn left and immediately right signed Little Wolford. Go straight through Little Wolford and on the outskirts of Great Wolford (2) follow the road to the right into the village. [4.3m/6.8km]

From Great Wolford take the road signed Todenham, and at T junction after 1m turn right back into Todenham (1). [1.2m/1.9km]

INFORMATION

1. TODENHAM   The village has a Tudor manor house. Much of the church is C14th; it has a Norman font and the chancel has a mediaeval cradle roof; there is an interesting memorial tablet on the outside South wall. [Ch PH]

2. GREAT WOLFORD   The earth works near the village are probably the remains of an iron age fort. The C19th church has a tall spire which is visible from a distance. [Ch PH]

Other PHs: Cherington.

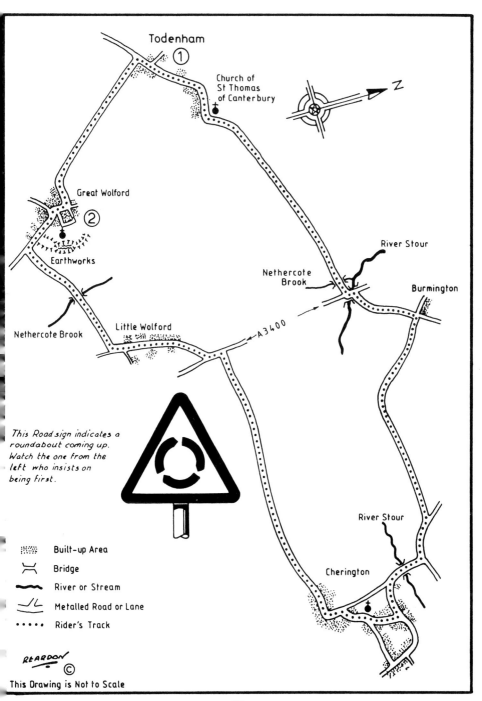

Todenham

①

Church of
St Thomas
of Canterbury

Z

Great Wolford

②

Earthworks

River Stour

Nethercote
Brook

Burmington

Nethercote Brook

Little Wolford

A3400

Nethercote
Brook

*This Road sign indicates a
roundabout coming up.
Watch the one from the
left who insists on
being first.*

River Stour

Cherington

Built-up Area

Bridge

River or Stream

Metalled Road or Lane

Rider's Track

REARDON ©

This Drawing is Not to Scale

INDEX

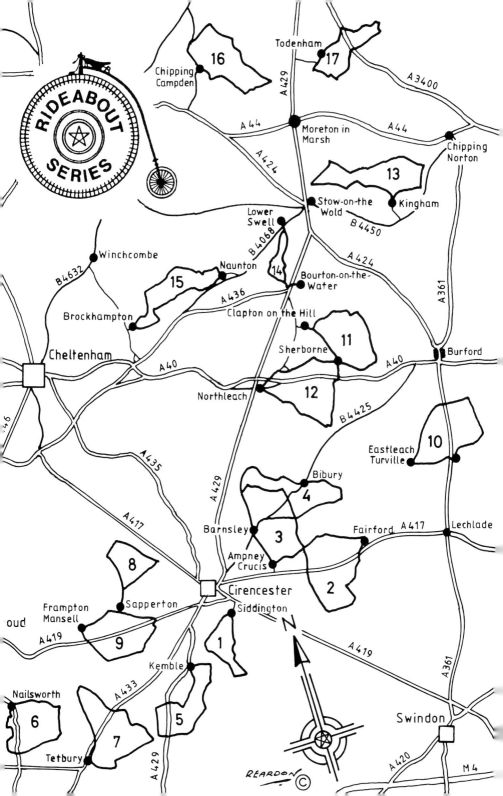

Cycle Hire in The Cotswolds

Nearest Town	Name	Tel
Bourton on the Water	Hartwells	01451 820405
Cheltenham	Compass Holidays	01242 250642
Cheltenham	Crabtree's	01242 515291
Cirencester	Pedal Power	01285 640505
Chipping Campden	Cotswold Country Cycles	01386 438706
Lower Swell	The Old Farmhouse Hotel	01451 830232
Moreton in Marsh	Country Lanes Cycle Centre	01608 650065
Moreton in Marsh	The Toy Shop	01608 650756
Tetbury	Thames & Cotswold	01666 503490

Tourist Information Centres

Broadway TIC	01386 852937
Cheltenham TIC	01242 522878
Chipping Campden TIC	01386 841206
Cirencester TIC	01285 654180
Gloucester TIC	01452 421188
Nailsworth TIC	01453 832532
Stow on the Wold TIC	01451 831082
Stroud TIC	01453 765768
Tetbury TIC	01666 503552
Tewkesbury TIC	01684 295027
Winchcombe TIC	01242 602925

Codes Used

C	=	Coffee
Ch	=	Church
D	=	Dovecote
F	=	Ford
M	=	Museum
PH	=	Public House or Inn
Sh	=	Shop
T	=	Toilets
TIC	=	Tourist Info Centre
Ts	=	Teas